the GLORIOUS CHRISTMAS

Darryl Quinn

SAMUEL PROPHESIED OF CHRIST'S BIRTH

Helaman 14:1-9

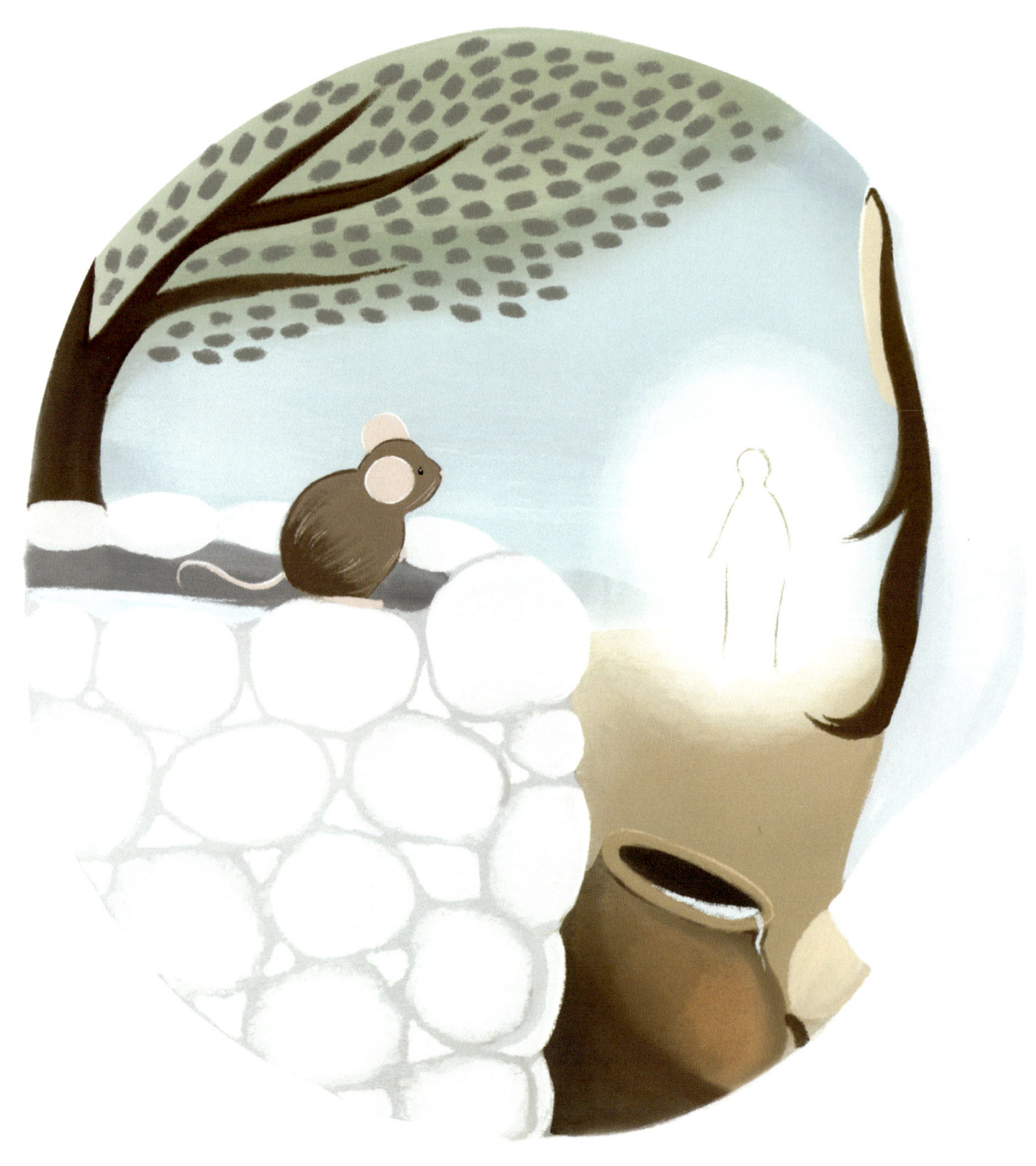

"FEAR NOT MARY"

Luke 1:29-33

Luke 1:26-27

MARY TOLD THOSE SHE LOVED

Luke 1:36-41

Matthew 1:20-21

JOSEPH LISTENED TO HEAVENLY FATHER'S WORDS AND HAD FAITH TO ACT

Matthew 1:24

CAESAR SENT OUT
A DECREE,
THAT ALL THE WORLD
SHOULD BE TAXED

Luke 2:1

JOSEPH WAS PREPARED TO SERVE HIS FAMILY

Luke 2:4-5

Luke 2:7

Luke 2:7

A NEW STAR TESTIFIED OF CHRIST'S BIRTH

Helaman 14:5

SHEPHERDS WERE KEEPING WATCH OVER THEIR FLOCK

Luke 2:8

Luke 2:9-12

"GLORY TO GOD"

Luke 2:13-14

Luke 2:16

THE SHEPHERDS TOLD OTHERS OF CHRIST'S BIRTH

Luke 2:17-20

Matthew 2:1-2

THE WISE MEN
TRAVELLED FAR
AND WORSHIPPED
BABY JESUS

Matthew 2:3

Matthew 2:11

SIMEON LOVED THE LORD AND GAVE THANKS

Luke 2:25-33

FOR MY CHILDREN

@thesundaysketchbook

ISBN 13: 978-1-4621-3962-0

Published by CFI, an imprint of Cedar Fort, Inc.
2373 W. 700 S., Springville, UT 84663
Distributed by Cedar Fort, Inc., www.cedarfort.com

Printed in the United States of America

10 9 8 7 6 5 4 3 2 1

Printed on acid-free paper